War Between the States

Harcourt
SCHOOL PUBLISHERS

Visit *The Learning Site!* **www.harcourtschool.com**

The North and the South

READ TO FIND OUT **Why did problems start between the Northern states and the Southern states?**

By the middle of the 1800s, the Northern states and the Southern states were very different. The North had a mixed economy. Some people worked on small farms. Many others worked in factories in cities.

In the South, almost everybody farmed. Large plantations used enslaved Africans to grow tobacco and cotton for sale. The North did not allow slavery.

The economy of the South was based mostly on farming.

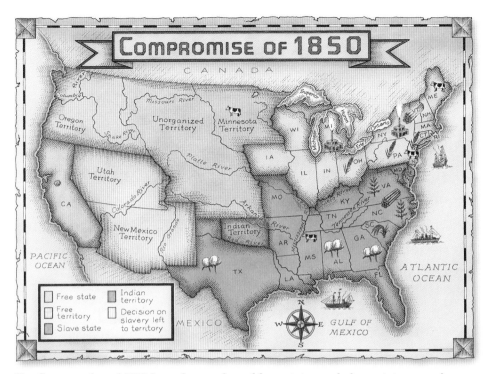

The Compromise of 1850 kept the number of free states and slave states equal for a while.

For a while, the country had the same number of free states as slave states. **Free states** did not allow slavery. **Slave states** did. Then people argued over whether new states should allow slavery. The Missouri Compromise and the Compromise of 1850 kept peace for a time.

The North did not like a law that said escaped slaves had to be sent back to their owners. The South did not like the high tax on goods from other countries.

READING CHECK ⏳ **GENERALIZE Why did problems start between the Northern states and the Southern states?**

Resisting Slavery

READ TO FIND OUT What groups of people worked against slavery?

Dred Scott was an enslaved man. His owner moved often. He took Scott with him. For a time, they lived in the North, where slavery was not allowed.

When his owner died, Scott went to court to fight for his freedom. He thought he should be free because he had lived on free land. In 1857, the Supreme Court said that slaves had no rights. This made the North and the South disagree even more over slavery.

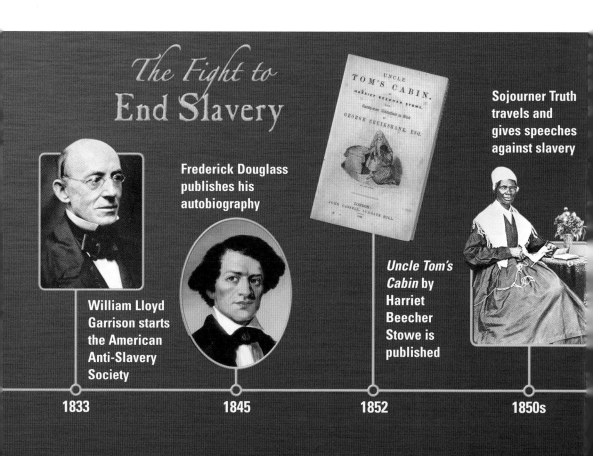

The Fight to End Slavery

Frederick Douglass publishes his autobiography

Sojourner Truth travels and gives speeches against slavery

William Lloyd Garrison starts the American Anti-Slavery Society

Uncle Tom's Cabin by Harriet Beecher Stowe is published

| 1833 | 1845 | 1852 | 1850s |

Routes on the Underground Railroad led slaves to freedom.

Many white Northern people and free African Americans worked against slavery. Some wrote newspaper articles and books. They told people why slavery was wrong. One famous book was *Uncle Tom's Cabin*.

Helping slaves escape on the Underground Railroad was another way people worked against slavery. The **Underground Railroad** was a set of secret routes that led to freedom. Most of the routes led to the north. Some led to Mexico.

READING CHECK **SUMMARIZE What groups of people worked against slavery?**

Harriet Tubman

"I never lost a passenger."

Harriet Tubman was born a slave. When she was 29 years old, she heard that her owner was going to sell her. She decided to escape instead.

Running away from her owner was very dangerous, but Harriet Tubman did it. She escaped to Philadelphia.

There, she thought about her friends and family who were still enslaved. She decided to help them escape, too. On her first try, Tubman led her sister and her sister's children to freedom.

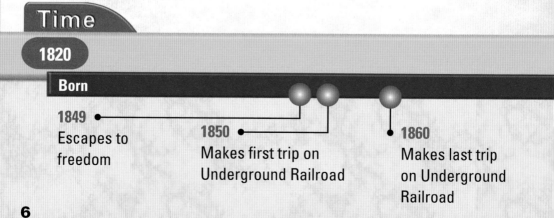

Time

1820

Born

1849
Escapes to
freedom

1850
Makes first trip on
Underground Railroad

1860
Makes last trip
on Underground
Railroad

Over time, Harriet Tubman made 18 more trips to the South. She helped more than 300 enslaved people escape.

Slave owners in the South wanted to stop Tubman. They offered to pay $40,000 to anyone who could capture her. Harriet Tubman became the most famous person working on the Underground Railroad. People all over the country knew about her. Some people called her Moses, after the man that the Bible says led people to freedom.

1911

Died

The Nation Divides

READ TO FIND OUT **What events broke apart the nation?**

In the 1850s, the country grew more divided over slavery. In 1859, John Brown and his followers tried to steal guns. They planned to give the guns to slaves so the slaves could fight for their freedom.

Brown was captured. He was put on trial and then hanged. In the North, many people called him a hero. This made people in the South sure that the North would do anything to end slavery.

John Brown hid in this building.

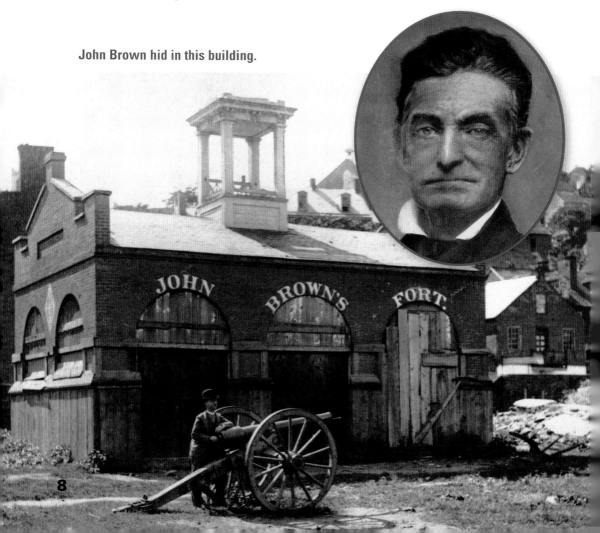

The United States in 1861

Union state
Border state
Confederate state
Territory

The Union states and the Confederate states

In 1860, Abraham Lincoln became President. He was against the spread of slavery into new states. Some Southern states voted to leave the Union, or the United States. They formed a new government called the **Confederacy**.

In April 1861, the Confederacy took over a United States fort on an island near South Carolina. With this attack, a civil war started. A **civil war** is a war between people in the same country.

READING CHECK SEQUENCE What events broke apart the nation?

The War Begins

READ TO FIND OUT **What were some important events in the early years of the war?**

The Union's plan to win the war was to keep the South from getting supplies. It tried to do this by blocking ports in the South. The Confederacy's plan was to fight until people in the North got tired of the war. The South hoped to get help from Britain and France.

The early battles showed that it would not be a quick war. After the battle of Antietam, President Lincoln said he would free the slaves in any area fighting against the Union.

The South planned to make the Civil War last a long time.

On January 1, 1863, Lincoln made his Emancipation Proclamation. To **emancipate** means "to free." From then on, as Union troops moved into the South, they freed enslaved people.

All kinds of people helped each side during the war. Some women took over the jobs that men left when they joined the army. Some worked as nurses, and some were spies. About 180,000 African Americans served in the Union army. They fought in almost every major battle.

READING CHECK **SEQUENCE What were some key events of the war's early years?**

The Battle of Bull Run

Toward a Union Victory

READ TO FIND OUT **How did the Union win the war?**

Several battles in 1863 changed the course of the war. In Mississippi, the Union army took over the city of Vicksburg on the Mississippi River. This cut the Confederacy in half.

At about the same time, the South won a battle in Virginia. This victory made Southern leaders think they could invade the North. When their army reached the town of Gettysburg, in Pennsylvania, Union troops met it. The armies fought for three days. In the end, it was a victory for the Union.

The siege of Vicksburg

General Lee (seated at left) surrenders to General Grant (seated at right).

In 1864, a Union army marched across the South. The army burned homes and crops along the way. At the same time, other Union troops captured the capital of the Confederacy. Soon the South's armies were out of food.

Finally, on April 9, 1865, the South gave up. More than 600,000 soldiers had died in the terrible war.

Five days after the war ended, President Lincoln was **assassinated**, or murdered. His death shocked the country.

READING CHECK ⓖ GENERALIZE How did the Union win the war?

Reconstruction

READ TO FIND OUT **How did Southern life change during Reconstruction?**

In his plan for **Reconstruction**, or rebuilding, of the nation, President Lincoln did not want to punish the South. The new President, Andrew Johnson, had a similar plan.

Some leaders in Congress thought that Johnson was too easy on the South. He let the Southern states pass laws that took away some of the rights of former slaves. Congress put the Southern states under military rule. It passed laws giving rights to African American citizens.

Congress wanted to punish the South for its part in the Civil War.

Reconstruction Plans	
Johnson's Plan	**Congress's Plan**
• Did not want to treat the Southern states too harshly	• Wanted to strictly punish the Southern states
• Supported the 13th Amendment to abolish slavery	• Supported the 13th Amendment to abolish slavery
• Southern states could have elections for state government	• Southern states would be under military rule
• State laws could limit rights of African Americans	• Supported the 14th Amendment, which assured equal citizenship rights
• Believed that states should decide who could and could not vote	• Supported the 15th Amendment, which assured voting rights for African American men

Many former slaves worked as sharecroppers.

Many African Americans were elected to government in the South. Life was still hard, however. Many formerly enslaved people went back to work on plantations. For pay, they kept part of the crops they grew. This was **sharecropping**. Even in good times, people made very little money from sharecropping.

Over time, Southern leaders passed laws to keep people separated by race. When Reconstruction ended, African Americans in the South again lost many of their rights.

READING CHECK ♨ GENERALIZE **How did Southern life change during Reconstruction?**

The Last Frontier

READ TO FIND OUT **Why did many people move west in the late 1800s?**

In the late 1800s, more gold and silver were discovered in the West. When someone found gold or silver, people rushed to that place from all over. Towns grew up quickly. They were wild places, with little law.

Some people moved west to build ranches. They wanted to raise cattle to sell in the cities of the East. They had to get their cattle to railroad centers to be taken east by train.

Mining towns were built very quickly.

Many homesteaders made homes out of sod. Sod is packed dirt held together by grass roots.

To get more people to move west, the government offered free land on the Great Plains. Anyone over the age of 21 could have a piece of land, or a homestead, if he or she lived on it for five years. Many thousands of people rushed to get their own land. These people were called **homesteaders**. Their life turned out to be very hard.

As more people moved west, Native Americans were forced to leave their land. The government made them live on land set aside for them.

READING CHECK SUMMARIZE **Why did many people move west in the late 1800s?**

New Industries

READ TO FIND OUT How did new industries and inventions change people's lives in the late 1800s?

In 1869, the first transcontinental railroad in the United States was finished. It linked the Atlantic and Pacific Coasts. For the first time, a person could go all the way across the country by train! Soon, more railroads were helping the country grow.

To make train tracks, steel mills were built. Soon, steel was also used to build tall buildings. They were called **skyscrapers** because they seemed to touch the sky.

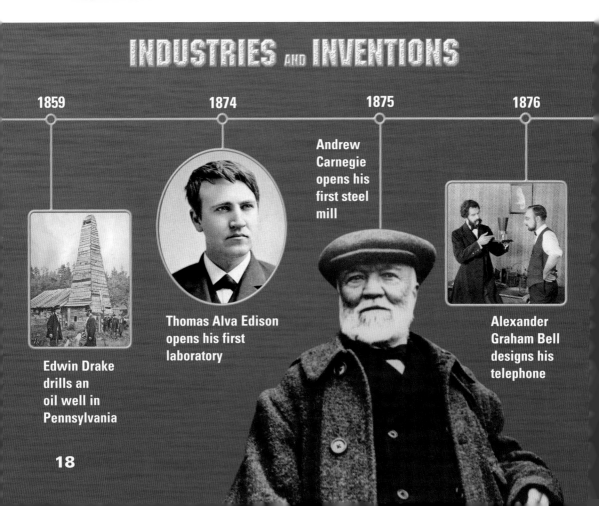

INDUSTRIES AND INVENTIONS

1859

Edwin Drake drills an oil well in Pennsylvania

1874

Thomas Alva Edison opens his first laboratory

1875

Andrew Carnegie opens his first steel mill

1876

Alexander Graham Bell designs his telephone

Many other inventions changed people's lives. Thomas Edison found ways to use electricity. In 1876, Alexander Graham Bell created a telephone. He started the country's first telephone company.

Some people became rich from these new ideas. Most people, however, worked very hard for very little money. Over time, they formed groups to fight for better working conditions. They wanted safer factories, shorter workdays, and fair pay.

READING CHECK ŏ **GENERALIZE How did new industries and inventions change people's lives in the late 1800s?**

1877

Edison invents the phonograph

Lewis Latimer invents a carbon filament lightbulb

1881

1883

The Brooklyn Bridge opens

1885

The Jenney Building opens in Chicago

Cities and Immigration

TIME Early 1900s
PEOPLE European immigrants
PLACE New York City

READ TO FIND OUT **What challenges did immigrants face?**

Between 1860 and 1910, millions of people came to the United States to live. They wanted freedom, safety, and a better life. Most came from southern and eastern Europe. Most had very little money. Many moved into crowded buildings called **tenements** in New York City.

A tenement neighborhood in New York City

Thousands of African Americans moved to northern cities.

Another large group of new people came from Asia. Many of them lived in San Francisco, California. Finding work and learning a new language were hard for the immigrants. Their neighborhoods were often dirty. Sometimes, other people treated them unfairly. Other people, however, offered them food, health care, and places to learn.

Between 1910 and 1930, thousands of African Americans moved from the South to cities in the North. They, too, were looking for a better life.

READING CHECK SUMMARIZE **What challenges did immigrants face?**

Activity 1

Write a term from the list to complete each sentence.

free state	tenement	homesteader
slave state	Confederacy	Reconstruction
emancipate	civil war	sharecropping
skyscraper	Underground Railroad	assassinated

1. A very tall building is a _____.

2. People cried when President Lincoln was _____.

3. There were no slaves in a _____ _____.

4. Slaves escaped by using the _____ _____.

5. It was not easy to run away from a _____ _____ and get to freedom.

6. A _____ was crowded with poor people who wanted to make a new life in the United States.

7. President Lincoln decided to _____ the enslaved people in the South.

8. After _____ ended, African Americans in the South lost many of their rights.

9. In a _____ _____, people from the same country fight against one another.

10. The soldiers of the _____ fought bravely.

11. A _____ rushed west to get his or her own land.

12. Former slaves made very little money from _____.

Activity 2

Look at the list of vocabulary words. Categorize the vocabulary words in a chart like the one below. Then use a glossary or dictionary to learn the definitions of the words that sound familiar or that you do not know.

sectionalism

tariff

secede

civil war

prejudice

Reconstruction

freedmen

segregation

bust

skyscraper

labor union

transcontinental railroad

collective bargaining

Underground Railroad

free state

states' rights

Confederacy

strategy

address

black codes

sharecropping

prospector

homesteader

petroleum

strike

slave state

fugitive

artillery

emancipate

assassinate

acquit

secret ballot

boom

reservation

tenement

reformer

settlement house

border state

		I Know	Sounds Familiar	Don't Know
○	sectionalism			✓
	secede		✓	
	skyscraper	✓		

Review

 Generalize Why did some Southern states leave the Union after Abraham Lincoln was elected President?

Vocabulary

1. How are the terms **slave state** and **Confederacy** related?

Recall

2. What caused conflict between the North and the South?
3. How did the South change during Reconstruction?
4. What challenges did immigrants face when they came to the United States?

Critical Thinking

5. Why do you think immigrants were often treated badly?

Activity

Design an Advertisement To attract people to the Great Plains, the railroads sometimes placed advertisements in newspapers. They offered low-cost land to settlers. Write and design an advertisement to get people to move to the Great Plains. In your ad, describe the benefits of living there.

Photo credits Front Cover Bettmann/Corbis; 8 (l) CORBIS; 8 (r) The Granger Collection, New York; 10 Bettmann/Corbis; 11 Don Troiani / Historical Image Bank; 12 Andy Thomas, Maze Creek Studio; 13 Library of Congress; 15 New York Historical Society; 16 Bettmann/Corbis